D1630737

ONE SECRET THING

Satan Says
The Dead and the Living
The Gold Cell
The Sign of Saturn: Poems 1980–87
The Father
The Wellspring
Blood, Tin, Straw
The Unswept Room
Selected Poems

ONE SECRET THING

Sharon Olds

CAPE POETRY

Published by Jonathan Cape 2009

2 4 6 8 10 9 7 5 3 1

First published in Great Britain in 2009 by
Jonathan Cape
Random House, 20 Vauxhall Bridge Road,
London SW1V 2SA

www.rbooks.co.uk

Addresses for companies within The Random House Group Limited can be found
at: www.randomhouse.co.uk/offices.htm

The Random House Group Limited Reg. No. 954009

A CIP catalogue record for this book is available from the British Library

ISBN 9780224087841

The Random House Group Limited supports The Forest Stewardship
Council (FSC), the leading international forest certification organisation.
All our titles that are printed on Greenpeace approved FSC certified paper
carry the FSC logo. Our paper procurement policy can be found at:
www.rbooks.co.uk/environment

Mixed Sources
Product group from well-managed
forests and other controlled sources
www.fsc.org Cert no. TT-COC-2139
© 1996 Forest Stewardship Council

Typeset in Bembo by Palimpsest Book Production Limited,
Grangemouth, Stirlingshire

Printed and bound in Great Britain by
MPG Books Ltd, Bodmin, Cornwall

CONTENTS

EVERYTHING

Most of us are never conceived.
Many of us are never born –
we live in a private ocean for hours,
weeks, with our extra or missing limbs,
or holding our poor second head,
growing from our chest, in our arms. And many of us,
sea-fruit on its stem, dreaming kelp
and whelk, are culled in our early months.
And some who are born live only for minutes,
others for two, or for three, summers,
or four, and when they go, everything
goes – the earth, the firmament –
and love stays, where nothing is, and seeks.

PART ONE
WAR

WAR

1. Woman with the Lettuce

They are crowded in a line being shoved toward a truck.
Some seem stunned, some sick with fear.
She stands slightly outside the line,
black hat clamped on her head,
mouth compressed. In her hands she holds
an oversized lettuce, its white stems and
great, pale, veined leaves
unfolded in the dense air. She stares
directly at the camera, the large, delicate
plant in her grip, its glowing vanes
reaching out. Furious, she takes her
last chance to look right at us.

2. Legless Fighter Pilot

He takes his right calf in his hand,
lifts the whole leg up, straight,
turns, and swings it into the cockpit,
sliding into the seat. The left leg he
bends by hand at the knee, pulls it in, and
slams the hatch, then in his aircraft
he rises over the hills. In the sky
no one can walk, everyone
is a sitting duck, he banks and begins to hunt.
He is not afraid of anything now,
not even his coffin – hell, he is part
native oak already, and if he
lost his arms he'd replace them. All he
wants is to bag as many as he can,
crash them into the ground like birds into a sack with their
useless legs trailing out the mouth of it.

3. What Could Happen

When the men and women went into hiding,
they knew what could happen if the others caught them.
They knew their bodies might be undone,
their sexual organs taken as if
to destroy the mold so the human could not
be made anymore. They knew what the others
went for – the center of the body,
and not just for the agony and horror but to
send them crudely barren into death,
throwing those bodies down in the village at dawn
to show that all was ended. But each
time the others dumped a body in the square,
a few more people took to the woods,
as if springing up, there,
from the loam dark as the body's wound.

4. The Dead

The ground was frozen, the coffin-wood burned
for fuel. So the dead were covered with something
and taken on a child's sled to the cemetery
in the subzero air. They lay on the snow,
some wrapped in rough cloth
bound with rope, like the tree's ball of roots
when it waits to be planted; others wound
in sheets, their gauze, tapered shapes
stiff as cocoons which will split down the center
when the new life inside is prepared;
but most lay like corpses, their coverings
coming loose, naked calves
hard as corded wood spilling
from under a tarp, a hand reaching out
as if to the bread made of glue and sawdust,
to the icy winter, and the siege.

5. When He Came for the Family

They looked at their daughter standing with her music
in her hand, the page covered with dots and
lines, with its shared language. They knew
families had been taken. What they did not know
was the way he would pick her cello up
by the scroll neck and take its amber
torso-shape and lift it and break it
against the fireplace. The brickwork crushed the
close-grained satiny wood, they stood and
stared at him.

6. The Signal

When they brought his body back, they told
his wife how he'd died:
the general thought they had taken the beach,
and sent in his last reserves. In the smokescreen,
the boats moved toward shore. Her husband
was the first man in the first boat
to move through the smoke and see the sand
dark with bodies, the tanks burning,
the guns thrown down, the landing craft
wrecked and floored with blood. In the path of the
bullets and shells from the shore, her husband had
put on a pair of white gloves
and turned his back on the enemy,
motioning to the boats behind him
to turn back. After everyone else
on his boat was dead
he continued to signal, then he, too,
was killed, but the other boats had seen him
and turned back. They gave his wife the medal,
and she buried him, and at night floated through
a wall of smoke, and saw him at a distance
standing in a boat, facing her,
the gloves blazing on his hands as he motioned her back.

7. The Leader

Seeing the wind at the airport blowing on his hair,
lifting it up where it was slicked down, you
want to say to the wind, Stop, that's
the leader's hair, but the wind keeps lifting it
and separating the thin strands and
fanning it out like a weed-head in the air.
His brows look bright in the airport glare,
his eyes are crinkled up against the sun, you
want to say to his eyes, Stop, you are
the leader's eyes, close yourselves, but they are
on his side, no part of his body
can turn against him. His thumbnail is long and
curved — it will not slit his throat for the
sake of the million children; his feet in their
polished shoes won't walk him into the
propeller and end the war. His heart won't
cease to beat, even if it knows
whose heart it is — it has no loyalty to
other hearts, it has no future outside his body.
And you can't suddenly tell his mind that it is
his mind, get out while it can,
it already knows that it's his mind —
much of its space is occupied with the
plans for the marble memorial statues
when he dies of old age. They'll place one
in every capital city of his nation
around the world — Lagos, Beijing,
São Paolo, New York, London, Baghdad,
Sydney, Paris, Jerusalem,
a giant statue of him, Friend to the Children
of the leader's country —
which will mean all children, then,
all those living.

8. The Smile

The man hunched on the ground, holding
the arm of the corpse, is smiling. And the man
bending over, stabbing the chest,
a look of pleasant exertion on his face,
is smiling. The man lying on the ground is
staring up, shirt splattered black
like splashes around a well where the bucket has been
dipped and dipped. They hold his wrists, as if
displaying his span, a large bird
slung from its heavy wing tips,
and the handsome young man goes on stabbing
and smiling, and the other sits on the ground
holding the dead arm like a leash, smiling.

9. Free Shoes

The pairs of shoes stand in rows,
polished and jet, like coffins for small pets,
lined with off-white. Evacuated children
sit in rows eyeing the pairs,
child after child after child, no parents
anywhere near. When it's their turn,
they get a pair of new shoes
and the old ones are taken away.

Of course it is kind of the nice people
to give them the shoes. Of course it is better
to be here in the country, not there where the buildings
explode and hurl down pieces of children.
Of course, of course. This life that has been
given them like a task! This life, this
black bright narrow unbroken-in shoe.

10. The Body-Sniffers

Eventually, they found the people
who could tell by the smell whether or not
someone was alive in the ruins. They would crouch,
move their heads above holes in the rubble,
and after a while they'd say Yes, there is something,
someone. They'd inhale some more,
lying flat on the planks, the odor
trickling up, into their brains, and
sometimes they'd say, It's too late, here.
Other times the blood was still flowing and
then the large beams would be hoisted, the
pipes cut, the bricks lifted,
foot by foot they'd go down and the sniffer would
say, Keep going, someone's there! They'd dig day and
night without sleep to see the eyelids
flutter, to smell the fresh, dissolved salt.

11. His Crew

Burning, he kept the plane up
long enough for the crew to jump. He could
feel the thrust down, and the lift,
each time one of them leapt, full-term, the
parachutes unfolding and glistening, little
sacs of afterbirth. They drifted toward
what could be long lives, his fist
seared to the stick. When he'd felt all six
leave him, he put the nose down
and saw the earth coming up toward him,
green as a great basin of water
being lifted to his face.

12. The Body

The body lies, dropped down on the stones,
pieces of plastic and steel in it, it is
not breathing, it cannot make its
heart pump no matter how hard it tries.
It tries to move its left hand,
its left foot − its lips, tongue,
it cannot cry, it cannot feel,
the lovely one is gone, the one who
rode it, rider on a mount, the one who had
a name and spoke. It lies on the rocks in its
camouflage, canteen at its belt,
probably still holding water,
and it can't do anything, it can't even
get at the water, they will put it in a pit,
cover it over, it will never feel
that vivid one
wake in it.

PART TWO
THE CANNERY

THE CANNERY, 1942–1945

When we'd visit it, down the street,
in the grammar school, I was so young
I sat on my mother's forearm, and gazed at the
stainless retort where the cylinders
of tinned iron and sheet metal,
hermetically sealed, glided, at a slant,
like a column of soldered soldiers, single-
file, down along the slatted chrome
ramp from the flame-sterilizers
in the requisitioned lunchroom. The woman
who ran that home-front cannery was
shorter than I from my perch, she was heavy, she had
short hair, and she moved with purpose,
there in her war-effort kitchen. I thought she had
invented the machine, and owned it, down would
soar, shoulder to shoulder, the ranks of
rations, as if we could see the clever
workings of her mind. When the war ended,
and the little factory was dismantled, she killed
herself. I didn't know what it meant,
what she had done, as if she had canned
her own spirit. I wish I could thank her
for showing me a woman Hephaistos
at her forge fire. My mother held me up
as if to be blessed by her. I wish her
heaven could have been the earth she had been desiring.

DIAGNOSIS

By the time I was six months old, she knew something
was wrong with me. I got looks on my face
she had not seen on any child
in the family, or the extended family,
or the neighborhood. My mother took me in
to the pediatrician with the kind hands,
a doctor with a name like a suit size for a wheel:
Hub Long. My mom did not tell him
what she thought in truth, that I was Possessed.
It was just these strange looks on my face —
he held me, and conversed with me,
chatting as one does with a baby, and my mother
said, She's doing it now! Look!
She's doing it now! and the doctor said,
What your daughter has
is called a sense
of humor. Ohhh, she said, and took me
back to the house where that sense would be tested
and found to be incurable.

AT NIGHT

At night my mother tucked me in, with a
jamming motion — her fingertips
against the swag of sheets and blankets
hanging down, where the acme angle of the
Sealy Posturepedic met
the zenith angle of the box spring — she shoved,
stuffing, doubling the layers, suddenly
tightening the bed, racking it one notch
smaller, so the sheets pressed me like a fierce
restraint. I was my mother's squeeze,
my mother was made of desire leashed.
And my sister and I shared a room —
my mother tucked me in like a pinch,
with a shriek, then wedged my big sister in, with a
softer eek, we were like the parts of a
sexual part, squeaky and sweet,
the room full of girls was her blossom, the house was my
mother's bashed, pretty ship, she
battened us down, this was our home,
she fastened us down in it, in her sight,
as a part of herself, and she had welcomed that part —
embraced it, nursed it, tucked it in, turned out the light.

BEHAVIOR CHART

There was one for each child, hand-ruled
with the ivory ruler – horizontal
the chores and sins, vertical
the days of the week. And my brother's and sister's
charts were spangled with gold stars,
as if those five-point fetlocks of brightness were
the moral fur they were curly with, young
anti-Esaus of the house, and my chart
was a mess of pottage marks, some slots filled
in so hard you could see where the No. 2
Mongol had broken – the rug under the grid
fierce with lead-thorns. My box score
KO, KO, I was Lucifer's knockout, yet it
makes me laugh now to remember my chart.
Affection for my chart?! As if I am looking
back on matter – my siblings' stars armed
figures of value, and my x'ed-out boxes
a chambered hatchery of minor
evils, spiny sea-stars, the small
furies of a child's cross tidal heart.

CALVINIST PARENTS

*Sometime during the Truman Administration, Sharon Olds's
parents tied her to a chair, and she is still writing about it.*
                              review of *The Unswept Room*

*My father was a gentleman, and he expected us to be gentle-
men. If we did not observe the niceties of etiquette he whopped
us with his belt. He had a strong arm, and boy did we feel it.*
                              Prescott Sheldon Bush, brother to
                              a president and uncle to another

They put roofs over our heads.
Ours was made of bent tiles,
so the edge of the roof had a broken look,
as if a lot of crockery
had been thrown down, onto the home –
a dump for heaven's cheap earthenware.
Along the eaves, the arches were like
entries to the Colosseum
where a lion might appear, or an eight-foot armored
being with the painted face
of a simpering lady. Bees would not roost
in those concave combs, above our rooms,
birds not swarm. How does a young 'un
pay for room and board? They put a
roof over our heads, against lightning,
and droppings – no foreign genes, no outside
gestures, no unfamilial words;
and under that roof, they labored as they had been
labored over, they beat us into swords.

MONEY

Filthy lucre, dough, lettuce,
jack, folderola, wherewithal, the ready,
simoleons, fins, tenners, I savored
the smell of money, sour, like ink,
and salty-dirty, like strangers' thumbs,
we touch it like our mutual skin
tattooed with webs – orb and ray – and with
Abe, and laurel leaves, and Doric
pillars, and urns, acanthus, mint scales,
a key. I liked the feel of it,
like old, flannel pajamas, the fiber
worn to a gloss, and the 2 x 6
classic size, which does not change
from generation unto generation as the
hand grows to encompass it –
and I liked the numerals, the curly
5, and the 1 the grandmother president
seems to be guarding,
as if the government would protect your identity
if they could find it, and they didn't have to kill
too many of your relatives
to get at it. Poor identity,
glad-handed so long, the triangle head all
eye, over the pyramid torso,
parent over child, rock OVER SCISSORS,
ANNUIT COEPTIS OVER NOVUS
ORDO SECLORUM. A dime a week
if you did your jobs and did not act morally
horrible, which meant, for some, a dime
a year. Now if my mom had paid me, to hit me,
I could have had a payola account,
and been a child whore magnate. No question
what it meant, to see the interest mount up,

the wad of indenture, legal tender –
no question to me what a bill was,
its cry sounded like the diesel train's
green cry, it was a ticket to ride.

FLY ON THE WALL IN THE
PURITAN HOME

And then I become a fly on the wall
of that room, where the corporal punishment
was done. The humans who are in it mean little
to me – not the offspring, nor the off-sprung –
I turn my back and with maxillae and palps
clean my arms: in each of the hundred
eyes of both my compound eyes,
one wallpaper rose. And if I turn back,
and the two-legged insect is over the lap
of the punishing one, the Venus trap,
I watch, and thrust my narrow hairy
rear into a flower at the rhythm the big one is
onward-Christian-soldiering and
marching-off-to-warring – as she's smoting,
I'm laying my eggs in the manure of a rose,
pumping to the beat. And my looking is a looking
primed, it is a looking to the power of itself,
and I see a sea folding inward,
200 little seas folding on themselves –
a mess of gene pool crushing down onto
its own shore. Then I turn back
to washing my hands of the chaff that flees off the
threshed onto the threshing floor.
Ho hum, I say, I'm just a flay –
fly light, fly bright, pieces of a species dashed
off onto a wall, chaff of wonder,
chaff of night.

MAIDEN NAME

Cobb: it's akin to Icelandic *kobbi,*
seal, and my father could float and fall
asleep on the water, and drift, steady
as a *male swan.* Dip down below gender, it's
a lump or piece of anything, as of
coal, ore, or stone – not ashes
but a clod – *usually of a large size*
but not too large to be handled by one person – as at
times, in my life, I have been a dazzled
rounded heap or mass of something being
glistened almost out of existence. *A cobnut*
was the boys', and *a testicle,* but not *the stone*
of a fruit – *especially a drupaceous fruit* –
or a peapod, or a small stack
of grain or hay, or a bunch of hair,
as a chignon – *or a small loaf*
of bread, a kind of muffin, a baked apple
dumpling! Oh father me, tuck me in.
I'll be the *stocky horse, one having an*
artificially high stylish action,
and gladly be the pabulum, *the*
string of crystals of sugar of milk,
$C_{12}H_{22}O_{11},$
separable from the whey, dextra-
rotatory, as one might search
through matter for matter one could like being made of.
A mixture consisting of unburned clay,
usually with straw as a binder,
for constructing walls of small buildings,
or matter leaping up like spirit,
a black-backed gull, or the eight-legged Jesus,
the *spider* – dear Dad, I search for how
to be your daughter, and I find the *wicker*
basket you liked to say you had carried me

around in. And now I want to cob your name
(to strike, to thump, specifically
to beat on the buttocks, as with a strap
or flat stick), O *young herring,*
O *head of a herring.* Dear old awful herring,
let's go back through *covetous*
to *thresh out seed*, let's go back
to *ore dressing,* to *break into pieces,*
break off the waste and low-grade materials –
it is sweet *to throw, especially gently*
or carelessly, to toss, as if
your carelessness had been some newfangled
gentleness. Your spirit lies in my
spirit this morning *crosswise, as timbers*
or logs in cobwork construction, as we *make*
or mend, coarsely, as I *patch* or *botch*
these *cobbl'd* rhymes.

MEN'S SINGLES, 1952

I sat in the noonday sun, no hat,
no comb, no braces, my teeth reaching out buck
naked toward food and drink, no breasts,
no fat — my first Finals by myself —
in front of us, as in the language of a dream,
grown men danced and rushed the net.
And something was building in my belly, some scaffold,
an edifice where the flesh of those half-bare
kings could sing, a green bleachers
of desire. One of them was elder, I rooted for his
shapely legs, their straight hair black —
my heart in the stands had a fierce fixation,
like a secret ownership, on him,
for his pins and his face, and his name which held
some key to knowledge, Vic Seixas. But when
the younger, big and tawny, would serve
with his back to me, then I could be
the ace, the golden tiger, the Schräber
Apollo, the Tony Trabert. I baked,
on the bleachers' slats, Arden bench
of cooked Arcadian wood, beside
a grown-up I did not know, and when he
came back, once, with a beer, he brought back
a Coke, for me — the varicose
brown-emerald bottle I had seen the magazine
pictures of, forbidden drink with
cocaine and dead men's fingers in it, I
drank, and cracked a sepia sweat —
Diana racing through the forest, the V of her
legs, at the top, as beautiful
as the power of a man, the nipples on her chest
pointing her to the hunt that makes death
worth it, Love/Nothing, Advantage In,
Let Ball, Take Two, the hush fell over us.

THE FLOAT

A Commanding Officer, after The War,
had given it to someone's father, who had
anchored it in the lake, a square
aluminum pontoon, seamed with solder.
I was a little postindustrial
water rat in a one-piece suit with the
Blue Willow pattern from a dinner plate on it,
the man on the left nipple going
away forever, the woman on the right
forever waiting. I would dive into the lake
– immediate, its cobalt reach and
silence – slide down, into the rich,
closed, icy book, blue lipped
in a white rubber cabbage-roses
headdress, and a coral rubber nose-clip,
slow-flitting like an agate-eating
swallow, floating sideways in
the indigo pressure. The grown-ups said we must
not, swim, under, the float,
we might get tangled in the anchor chain, I
swam, under the float, and saw
the slant of the chain, its mottled eel. And you must
never go up, under the raft, to its
recessed chamber where there's poison ether.
I would soar supine on my back, looking up
at the bulk, I'd rush up slowly closer
to the antilife, holding my breath,
finally dipping up into it,
putting my face up into it
a second or two, then shove down
and water-sprint for home. But of course
I felt I had to inhale that stuff
and live. I left no note, the woman on my
right chest would always long for

the man on my left, and never touch him, I
came up, between those boiler-plated
bulges, and breathed. It was more an unguent
than air, it smelled like myrrh gone bad,
I'd go and sip it up all summer,
and live. Sip, sip, sip,
first the left, then the right
nipple faintly puffed, almost
chartreuse with silvery newness, the lover
on the left pushed out his mouth, and on the right
she puckered hers – if they grew enough,
they could kiss, or some resuscitator could be
begged to give them mouth to mouth to mouth.

FREEZER

When I think of people who kill and eat people,
I think of how lonely my mother was.
She would come to me for comfort, in the night,
she'd lie down on me and pray. And I could say
she fattened me, until it was time
to cook me, but she did not know,
she'd been robbed of a moral sense that way.
How soft she was, how unearthly her beauty, how
terrestrial the weight of her flesh
on the constellation of my joints and pouting
points. I like to have in the apartment,
shut in a drawer, in another room,
the magazine with the murder-cannibal,
it comforts me that the story is available
at any moment, accounted for, not
dangerously unthought-of. I think he kept
ankles in the freezer. My mother was such a good kisser.
From where I sat in the tub, her body,
between her legs, looked a little
like a mouth, a youthfully bearded mouth
with blood on it. From one hour to the next on earth
no one knew what would happen.

THE BRA

It happened, with me, on the left side, first,
I would look down, and the soft skin of the
nipple had become like a blister, as if it had been
lifted by slow puffs of breath
from underneath. It took weeks, months,
a year. And those white harnesses,
like contagion masks for conjoined twins
— if you saw a strap showing, on someone
you knew well enough, you could whisper, in her ear,
It's Snowing Up North. There were bowers to walk through
home from school, trellis arches
like aboveground tunnels, froths of leaves —
that spring, no one was in them, except,
sometimes, a glimpse of police. They found
her body in the summer, the girl in our class
missing since winter, in the paper they printed
the word in French, *brassiere*, I felt a little
glad she had still been wearing it,
as if a covering, of any
kind, could be a hopeless dignity.
But now they are saying that her bra was buried
in the basement of his house — when she was pulled down into
the ground, she was naked. For a moment I am almost half
glad they tore him apart with Actaeon
electric savaging. In the photo,
the shoulder straps seem to be making
wavering O's, and the sorrow's cups
are O's, and the bands around to the hook
and eye in the back make a broken O.
It looks like something taken down
to the bones — God's apron — God eviscerated —
its plain, cotton ribbons rubbed
with earth. When he said, In as much as ye have
done it unto one of the least
of these my brethren, ye have done it unto
me, he meant girls — or if he'd known better
he would have meant girls.

33

THE COULDN'T

And then, one day, though my mother had sent me
upstairs to prepare, my thumbs were no longer
opposable, they would not hook into
the waistband, they swung, limp – under my
underpants was the Y of elastic, its
metal teeth gripping the pad,
I couldn't be punished, unless I was bare, but I
couldn't be bare, unless I took off my
Young Lady's First Sanitary Belt,
my cat's cradle, my goddess girdle,
and she couldn't want me to do that,
could she? But when she walked in, and saw me still
clothed, her face lit up with sarcastic
wonder, and combat. I did not speak, she came
toward me, I bolted, threw open her door,
slamming my brother to the floor with a keyhole
shiner, I poured down the staircase and through
some rooms, and got my back against
a wall, I would hurt her before the last scene
of this long-running act could be played out
to its completion. When she got there, maybe she could see that,
we faced off, dressed in our dresses and our
secret straps and pulleys, and then
I walked away – and for the year I remained
in that house, each month our bodies called
to each other, brought each other bleeding off in the
waste of the power of creation.

HOME THEATER, 1955

They weren't armadillos, or sow bugs,
or nautili, the animals printed on the
seersucker cotton of my nightie, maybe they were
rabbits, or deer. There was a new style,
that year, the shortie nightie, no longer
than the hem of its matching panties – and on its
cloth no eels, no trilobites,
no oviraptors, but goldfish and pigs
placed in rows like sown seeds.
That night, what was supposed to be
inside our father's head – the arterial
red – had emerged and cooled on his brow,
cheeks, mouth, into a Comus mask,
and the police were there, and our mother was not. It was
like a Greek play, in a stone
amphitheater, with very few characters –
first the one in blood disguise,
then the elder daughter who
had called the two officers
to our home – they were not much older than she, they were
dressed for the hour in midnight blue.
And my sister's torso, in its shortie, in the kitchen,
seemed to be almost rippling,
swaying like an upright snake still
half in its basket. Then, for an instant,
I thought I saw the younger cop just
glance at my legs and away, once
and away, and for a second, the little
critters on my nightie seemed to me to be
romping as if in an advertisement.
Soon after our father had struck himself down,
there had risen up these bachelors
beside the sink and stove, and the tiny
mastodons, and bison, and elk, the
beasts on my front and back, began,
atonal, as if around an early fire, to chant.

PATERFAMILIAS

In the evenings, during the cocktail hour,
my mother's new husband would sometimes inspect
the troops. Your mother has the best damn fanny
in the house, he would say to my sister and me — in our
teens, then twenties, thirties, forties. Turn
around! he'd cry out, Turn around! We wouldn't
turn around, and he'd say, Your mother has the nicest little
ass in the house. And let's look at those legs,
he'd shout, and she'd flash her gams. Your mother
has the only decent legs in the house,
he'd growl. And when I'd pass him next,
he'd bear-hug me, as if to say
No hard feelings, and hit me hard
on the rear, and laugh very loud, and his eyes seemed to
shine as I otherwise never saw them shine,
like eyes of devils and fascists in horror
comic books. Then he'd freshen his Scotch, and just
top hers up, a little, and then
he'd show us his backwards-curled, decurved
Hohenzollern thumb — Go on,
touch it! Touch it! They were people who almost
did not know any better, who, once
they found each other, were happy, and felt,
for the first time, as if they belonged
on earth — maybe owned it, and every creature on it.

EASTER 1960

The doctor on the phone was young, maybe on his
first rotation in the emergency room.
On the ancient boarding-school radio,
in the attic hall, the announcer had given my
boyfriend's name as one of two
brought to the hospital after the sunrise
service, the egg-hunt, the crash — one of them
critical, one of them dead. I was looking at the
stairwell banisters, at their lathing,
the necks and knobs like joints and bones,
the varnish here thicker here thinner — I had said
Which one of them died, and now the world was
an ant's world: the huge crumb of each
second thrown, somehow, up onto
my back, and the young, tired voice
said my fresh love's name. It would have been
nice to tear out the balusters, and rail, and the
stairs, like a big backbone out of a
brontosaur, to take some action,
to do, and do, and do, as a done-to, and
dear one to a done-to-death-to, to have run, on a
treadmill, all night, to light the dorm,
the entire school, with my hate of fate,
and blow its wiring, and the town's wiring,
pull the wires of Massachusetts
out of the switchboard of the country. I went back to my
room, I did not know how to get
out of the world, or how to stay —
I sat on the floor with the Sunday *Times*
and read the columns of the first page down,
and then the next, and then the next.
I can still see how every *a*,
initiator of his given name,
looked eager — it hadn't heard, yet, that its

boy was gone – and every *f*
hung down its head on its broken neck,
its little arms held out, as if to
say, *You see me, this is what I am.*

PART THREE
UMBILICUS

UMBILICUS

When she was first in the air, upside down,
it linked us, the stem on which she had blossomed.
And they tied a knot in it, finishing
the work of her making. The limp remnant –
vein, and arteries, and Jelly of Wharton – had
lived as it would shrivel, by its own laws,
in a week it would wither away, while the normal
fetal holes in her heart closed,
the foramen ovale shutting the passage
the placental blood had swept, when her lungs,
flat in their dog-eared wet, had slept.
I was in shock, my life as I had known it
over. When they sent us home, they said
to bathe the stump in alcohol
twice a day. I was stone afraid,
and yet she was so interesting –
moist, doubled-up, wondering, undersea
being. And the death-nose at the belly-center wizened
and pizzled and ginsenged and wicked-witch'd until
the morning I undid her pajamas, and there, in the
night's cereus petals, lay her stamen,
in its place, on her, the folded tent,
imbliu, nabhila, nafli, at last
purely hers, toward the womb an eye
now sightless, now safe in moated memory.

WHEN OUR FIRSTBORN SLEPT IN

My breasts hardening with milk – little seeps
leaking into the folded husband
hankies set into the front curves
of the nursing harness – I would wander around
the quiet apartment when her nap would last a little
longer than usual. When she was awake, I was
purpose, I was a soft domestic
prowling of goodness – only when she slept
was I free to think the thoughts of one
in bondage. I had wanted to be someone – not just
someone's mom, but someone, some *one*.
Yet I know that this work that I did with her
lay at the heart of what mattered to me – was
that heart. And still there was a part of me
left out by it, as if exposed on a mountain
by mothering. And when she slept in,
I smelled the husks of olive rind
on that slope, I heard the blue knock
of the eucalyptus locket nut, I
tasted the breath of the wolf seeking
the flesh to enrich her milk, I saw the
bending of the cedar under the sea
of the wind – while she slept, it was as if
my pierced ankles loosed themselves
and I walked like a hunter in the horror-joy
of the unattached. Girl of a mother,
mother of a girl, I paced, listening,
almost part-fearing, sometimes, that she might have stopped
breathing, knowing nothing was anything, for me,
next to the small motions as she woke,
light and wind on the face of the water.
And then that faint cry, like a
pelagic bird, who sleeps in flight, and I would
turn, pivot on a spice-crushing heel,
and approach her door.

TOTH FARRY

In the back of the drawer, in the sack, the baby
canines and incisors are mostly chaff,
by now, no whole utensils left:
half an adze; half a shovel – in its
handle, a marrow well of the will
to dig and bite. And the enamel hems
are sharp as shell-tools, and the colors go
from salt, to pee on snow. One cuspid
is like the tail of an ivory chough,
I think it's our daughter's, but the dime hermes
mingled the chompers of our girl and boy, safe-
keeping them together with the note that says
*Der Toth Farry, Plees Giv Me
A Bag Of Moany.* I pore over the shards
like a skeleton lover – but who could throw out
these short pints of osseous breast-milk,
or the wisdom, with its charnel underside,
and its dome, smooth and experienced,
ground in anger, rinsed in silver
when the mouth waters. From above, its knurls
are a cusp-ring of mountaintops
around an amber crevasse, where in high
summer the summit wildflowers open
for a day – Crown Buttercup, Alpine Flames,
Shooting Star, Rosy Fairy Lantern,
Cream Sacs, Sugar Scoop.

HOME EC

It is an art, a craft, a kind of Home
Ec, slowly pulling out the small
rubber dome, this time almost
full of blackish blood. It is
like war, or surgery, without weapons
or instruments. The darkness of it
has the depth of truth. The clots are shocking and
thrilling in their shapes. I do what some
might do in their last days, knowing they will
never have another chance,
I rub my palms with it, and I want
to go across my face once, in ritual
streaks, but my glasses are on, and I'm in
a slight panic, seeing my reddened
life-lines. For a moment, while I still can,
I want to eat a dot of it,
but not the bitterness of spermicide,
or a sperm dead of spermicide.
Many millions have been killed today –
I hold my hands out to the mirror
over the sink, a moment, like a killer
showing her nature. Then left hand
to hot, right to cold, I turn on
the taps. And blood turns out to be flecks
suspended in water, the washy down
of a red hen. I feel that the dead
would be glad to come back for one moment of this,
in me the dead come back for a moment
to the honor and glory.

THE SPACE HEATER

On the ten-below-zero day, it was on,
the round-shouldered heater near the analyst's couch,
at its end, like the child's headstone which appeared
a year later, in the neighboring plot, near
the foot of my father's grave. And it was hot, with the
laughing satire of a fire's heat,
the little coils like hairs in Hell.
And it was making a group of sick noises –
I wanted the doctor to turn it off
but I couldn't seem to ask, so I just
stared, but it did not budge. The doctor
turned his heavy, soft palm
outward, toward me, inviting me to speak, I
said, 'If you're cold – are you cold? But if it's on
for me . . .' He held his palm out toward me,
I tried to ask, but I only muttered,
but he said, 'Of course,' as if I had asked,
and he stood and approached the heater, and then
stood on one foot, and threw himself
toward the wall with one hand, and with the other hand
reached down behind the couch, to pull
the plug out. I looked away,
I had not known he would have to bend
like that. And I was so moved, that he
would act undignified, to help me,
that I cried, not trying to stop, but as if
the moans made sentences which bore
some human message. If he would cast himself toward the
outlet for me, as if bending with me
in some old shame, then I would put my trust
in his art – and the heater purred, like a creature
or the familiar of a creature, or the child of a familiar,
the father of a child, the spirit of a father,
the healing of a spirit, the vision of healing,
the heat of vision, the power of the heat,
the pleasure of the power.

BARBAROUS ARTIFACTS

The execution building at each prison is nicknamed
after the equipment it houses.

In a pan of Joy and cold boiled water
lay the gloves I'd picked up, for some reason, off the street,
  in the sleet —
one large left, one huge right,
like gauntlets of centurions. I ran
in more hot, and coils of wool
surged out, tar pellets, facets of glass,
and there at the bottom was the six-inch spike I had
lifted from the excavation site.
And the spike was too heavy for its four-sided length
and thickness, like a piece of railroad steel
sixteen ounces on its home planet,
16 tons here. It had
a wavy shape, as if poured when hot, and we have
heard the scream when such a nail
is pulled from a human hoof. And the shaft looked
bitten, and the tip curled up like a talon,
and the head was bent down and dented. It looked old
as Rome, and the right size, but Jesus's
hands would have torn right through, they had nailed him
by his wrists, they didn't have the chair, yet,
with its scarlet cap, they didn't have the ovens
for him and his family. I set the gloves
on the daily news, to dry — one lost from one
worker, one lost from another, a left
and a right, the way we are in this together.
What a piece of work is man,
in Albany, and Washington,
in Texas, and in Louisiana, at
Angola, in the Red Hat House.

ANIMAL DRESS

The night before she went back to college,
she went through my sweater drawer, so when she left she
   was in
black wool, with maroon creatures
knitted in, an elk branched across her
chest, a lamb on her stomach, a cat,
an ostrich. Eighteen, she was gleaming with a haze
gleam, a shadow of the glisten of her birth
when she had taken off my body — that thick coat, cast
off after a journey. In the elevator
door window, I could see her half-profile —
strong curves of her face, like the harvest
moon, and when she pressed 1,
she set. Hum and creak of her descent,
the backstage cranking of the solar system,
the lighted car sank like a contained
calm world. Eighteen years
I had been a mother! In a way now I was past it —
resting, watching our girl bloom.
And then she was on the train, in her dress
like a zodiac, her body covered with
the animals that carried us in their
bodies for a thousand centuries
of sex and death, until flesh knew itself, and spoke.

ROYAL BEAUTY BRIGHT

After her toxic shock, my mother tried to
climb out of bed in the I.C.U. – half
over the rails, she'd dangle, the wires and
tubes holding her back, I.V.,
oxygen, catheter, blood-pressure cuff,
heart monitor – streaming with strings,
she'd halt, ninety pounds, and then she'd
haul, and the wires and tubes would go taut
and start to rip. So they tied her down,
first her chest in a soft harness,
strapped around the mattress, then her wrists
with long, sterile gauze ribbons,
to the bars of the bed, then, when she kicked until
she raised blue baby-fist welts on her ankles they
put her in five-point. I stood by the bed while she
bucked and tugged, she slowly raised her
head and shoulders like the dead, she called in a
hoarse, cold baritone,
Untie my hands. I sat by the rails,
she was fixed like a constellation to the bed,
and I sang to her, while the Valium
did nothing, not the first shot
or the second, I went through the old carols as she
squirmed and writhed, five-pointed flesh that
gave me life, and when the morphine took her,
I sang her down – Star of wonder,
Star of night.

SELF-EXAM

They tell you it won't make much sense, at first,
you will have to learn the terrain. They tell you this
at thirty, and fifty, and some are late
beginners, at last lying down and walking
the bright earth of the breasts – the rounded,
cobbled, ploughed field of one,
with a listening walking, and then the other –
fingertip-stepping, divining, north
to south, east to west, sectioning
the low, fallen hills, sweeping
for mines. And the matter feels primordial,
unimaginable – dense,
cystic, phthistic, each breast like the innards
of a cell, its contents shifting and changing,
streambed gravel under walking feet, it
seems almost unpicturable, not
immemorial, but nearly un-
memorizable, but one marches,
slowly, through grave or fatal danger,
or no danger, one feels around in the
two tackroom drawers, ribs and
knots like leather bridles and plaited
harnesses and bits and reins,
one runs one's hands through the mortal tackle
in a jumble, in the dark, indoors. Outside –
night, in which these glossy ones were
ridden to a froth of starlight, bareback.

THE RISER

When I heard that my mother had stood up after her near
death of toxic shock, at first
I could not get that supine figure in my
mind's eye to rise, she had been so
flat, her face shiny as the ironing board's
gray asbestos cover. Once my
father had gone that horizontal, he did
not lift up, again, until he was
fire. But my mother put her fine legs
over the side, got her soles
on the floor, slowly poured her body from the
mattress into the vertical, she
stood between nurse and husband, and they let
go, for a second – alive, upright,
my primate! When I'd last seen her, she was silver
and semi-liquid, like something ladled
onto the sheet, early form
of shimmering life, amoeba or dazzle of
jism, and she'd tried to speak, like matter
trying to speak. Now she stands by the bed,
gaunt, slightly luminous, the
hospital gown hanging in blue
folds, like the picture of Jesus-come-back
in my choir book. She seemed to feel close to Jesus,
she loved the way he did not give up,
nothing could stop his love, he stood there
teetering beside the stone bed and he
folded his grave-clothes.

WOODEN ODE

Whenever I see a chair like it,
I consider it: the no arms,
the lower limbs of pear or cherry.
Sometimes I'll take hold of the back slat
and lift the four-legged creature off the floor to hear
the joints creak, the wind in the timbers,
hauling of keel rope. And the structure will not
utter, just some music of reed and tether,
Old Testament cradle. Whenever I see
a Hitchcock chair — not a Federal,
or an Eames — I pay close, furniture
attention, even as my mind is taking its
seablind cartwheels back. But if every
time you saw a tree — pear,
cherry, American elm, American
oak, beech, bayou cypress —
your eyes checked for a branch, low enough
but not too low, and strong enough,
and you thought of your uncle, or father, or brother,
third cousin twice removed
murdered on a tree, then you would have
the basis for a working knowledge of American History.

THE SCARE

There was a cut clove of garlic, under
a glass tumbler, there were spoons tarnished opal
in a cup, there was a nesting bowl
in a nesting bowl in a nesting bowl
on the sill, when I understood there was a chance they might
have to remove my womb. I bent over,
wanting to cry out, It's my best friend, it's like
having a purse of your own, of yourself, it's like
being where you came from, as if you are your origin,
the basket of life, the withies, the osier
reed weave, where your little best beloveds
lay and took heart, took on the weights
and measures. I love the pear shape,
the upside-downness, the honor of bringing
forth the living so new they can almost
not be said to be dying yet.
And the two who rested, without fear or elation,
against the endometrium,
over the myometrium, held
around by the serosa . . . In the latter days,
the unclosed top of the precious head pressed
down on the inner os, and down on the
outer os, and the feet played up against
the fundus, and I could feel, in myself –
of myself – the tale of love's flesh.
Soon enough, the whole small
city of my being will demolish – what if now
one dwelling, the central dwelling,
the holy-seeming dwelling, might go. Like a fiber
suitcase, in a mown field, it stands,
its worn clasps gleaming.

PANSY CODA

When I see them, my knees get a little weak.
I have to squat down close to them, I
want to put my face in one of them.
They are so buttery, and yet so clean.
They have a kind of soaking-wet dryness,
they have the tremulous chin, and the pair of
ocular petals, and the pair of frail
ear petals, the sweet dog face.
Or is it like the vulva of a woman,
or of some particular woman. My mother
tended them — purple-black —
when I kneel to them I am kneeling to my mother,
who quietly shows her body to me
whenever it can be done with the slightest pretense of dignity,
as if it might be a pleasure to me.
She'll call to me, and when I come to her door
she'll walk across her room slowly,
eyes focused in front of her feet
but the corners of her eyes alert. She is so lonely
since her husband died, she just wants to be
naked in a room with someone, anyone,
but her face has something eerie in its blankness,
the eyes kept rounded — I have no idea
what she is thinking, I get that nervous feeling
I've had all my life around my mother. But when I
see a bed of these, I kneel,
and gaze at each one, freshly and freshly wowed,
I love to run my thumb softly
over the gentle jaw, I would like
to wrap myself in a cloak of them,
a cloak of one if it were large enough.
I am tired of hating myself, tired
of loathing. I want to be carried in a petal
sling, sling of satin and cream,
I want to be dazed, I want the waking sleep.

LAST WORDS, DEATH ROW, CIRCA 2030

I am one of the ones, here,
who did what I am said to have done.
Look to yourselves – I was conceived the month
you voted him in – look to the high
court which went for execution
and against abortion. You sentenced me
to this life lived out till tomorrow. And all
those people I killed, they'd be with you now,
if you'd let me die before I breathed,
when my mother and father needed me to die.
Would it have seemed more American to you if it
could have been a more public demise,
like this, if there could have been televised crowds
chanting outside the clinic, the cervix
magnified, on a drive-in screen,
the fetus me six feet tall
strapped to the table? Not that I
have a say in this – not tonight,
and not at eight o'clock tomorrow
morning, when I will be one of the dead
at last – how you have made me work for it.

SELF-PORTRAIT, REAR VIEW

At first, I do not believe it, in the hotel
triple mirror, that that is my body, in
back, below the waist, and above
the legs — the thing that doesn't stop moving
when I stop moving.
And it doesn't look like just one thing,
or even one big, double thing
— even the word saddlebags has a
smooth, calfskin feel to it,
compared to this compendium
of net string bags shaking their booty of
cellulite fruits and nuts. Some lumps
look like bonbons translated intact
from chocolate box to buttocks, the curl on top
showing, slightly, through my skin. Once I see what I can
do with this, I do it, high-stepping
to make the rapids of my bottom rush
in ripples like a world wonder. Slowly,
I believe what I am seeing, a 54-year-old
rear end, once a tight end,
high and mighty, almost a chicken butt, now
exhausted, as if tragic. But this is not
an invasion, my cul-de-sac is not being
used to hatch alien cells, ball peens,
gyroscopes, sacks of marbles. It's my hoard
of treasure, my good luck, not to be
dead, yet, though when I flutter
the wing of my ass again, and see,
in a clutch of eggs, each egg,
on its own, as if shell-less, shudder, I wonder
if anyone has ever died,
looking in a mirror, of horror. I think I will
not even catch a cold from it,
I will go to school to it, to Butt

Boot Camp, to the video store, where I saw, in the window, my hero, my workout jelly role model, my apotheosis: *Killer Buns.*

THE DEAD

When I ask my mother if she can remember
if my best friend, when I was nine,
died before, or after, her mother —
they had sprayed their tree with lead paint
in their closed garage — my mother describes
how furious my friend's father was,
years later, when my mother and her second
husband beat him and his second wife
in the waltz contest. Her voice is melodious,
she loves to win, her rival's loss
an erotic sweet. For a moment I see
it would not be an entirely bad thing
if my mother died. How interesting
to be in the world when she was not — how
odd to breathe air she would not recently
have breathed. I even envision her dead,
for a second — on her back, naked, like my father
small, my father as a woman, her mouth
open, as his was. Suddenly, I feel
not afraid — as if no one will hurt me.
And they're together again, a moment — a bridal
pair of things, a tongs! As if they
delivered me like a message then were put to death.
They cannot unmake me. I can safely thank them
for my life. Thank you for my life.

SLEEVES

for Edmund White

When Edmund said he is going to Hawaii
I was back there, 14 and never been kissed,
and the young man I liked had asked me to go
for a walk that evening on the beach. And what filled
my mind, all day, were the arm-holes
of his short-sleeved bright-flowered cotton shirt, those
circles which seemed of the diameter
of a pie tin – how would my hands, reaching
to go around him as he began to hug me, not
slip, like burrow mammals, into
those openings, not go to ground?
And the man was, I was telling Edmund,
the man was, what is it called, biff,
boff – buff, Edmund said –
the young man was a lifeguard
and a surfer, on the hard dune of each breast a
nipple like a tiny scatter of sand,
bits of coral and starfish. And of course
my fear was desire, to pour, up,
into him, and into myself, and
swim, and strike together for the shore
– where we stood, later, in the late evening, and his
arms opened, and my arms opened,
and the origami closed itself
around the delicate, shut kiss.
And the air smelled of plumeria
and frangipani – when the plane door
opens, you will smell it! And Edmund said,
You know what homosexuals
are called in China? Cut Sleeves –
when the emperor's lover fell asleep
in his arms, and lay sleeping on the silk of the royal

robe, and the emperor had to get up,
he cut off the sleeve of his gown, so as not
to wake the young man, but leave him in the deeps of his
    dream.

GOOD MEASURE

Something wakes me, at my mother's house,
in the dark. On the back of my hand, a luminous
wedge, a patch of Alamogordo –
the new-risen moon, the last quarter,
as if my mother, in her sleep, took
a ladle, and poured this portion. Now that
my mother loves me, I feel a little
cheated – who will be true, anymore,
to the years of drought? Whoever will
be true to them can thirst in good measure
under the glistening breast. There used to be no
choice, for her, she was a gurdy
of atoms swinging from each other's elbows,
a force of hurdy wolvine cream,
and then, later, there was choice, she could dwell
on herself in bitterness, or dwell on
herself in hope. But sometimes, lately, there's a
motion, diurnal – when drenched with attention
she might turn to me, with affection – that's when I
feel that sore resentful rib.
They call the half moon the last
quarter, staying faithful to the back bulge,
to the edge between too little and too much,
the narrow calcium line neither roasting
nor freezing – as if one could make one's home
on that border, if one could just keep moving,
nomad offspring of the stone opal
wanderer who is borne, singing,
across the night. My mother loves me
with a full, child's heart. Here is my pleynt.

PART FOUR
CASSIOPEIA

CASSIOPEIA

1. He Is Taken Away

When they'd put her husband in the ambulance,
my mother stood beside it, looking into
its lighted window. It was midnight, the moon
like a larva high against the trunk
of the sequoia. The distant neighboring houses
were dark, the flowering shrubs dark,
I brought the car around, and she was
standing there, looking in that horizontal
picture window. I had never seen her so
still, yet she looked so alive, so vivid,
like a woman motionless at the moment of orgasm,
pure attention. She was glowing, slightly,
from the inner ambulance light, she seemed to
have no outside or inside, her surface
all depth,
every cell of her body was looking at him.
Doors slammed, I called to her, she
turned to me, like a scrimshaw Crusader
chess-piece rotated slowly on its base,
she called in response, melodious,
looking nowhere near me, she was
made of some other material,
wax or ivory or marble, she looked like
Homer ready to be led around the known globe.

2. The Music

On the phone my mother says she has been sorting
her late darling's clothes – *and it BREAKS
my HEART,* and then there are soft sounds,
as if she's been lowered down, into
a river of music. *I'm not unhappy,*
she says, *this is better for me than church,*
her voice through tears like the low singing
of a watered plant long not watered,
she lets me hear what she feels. I could be in a
cradle by the western shore of a sea, she could
be a young or an ancient mother.
Now I hear the melody
of the one bound to the mast. It had little
to do with me, her life, which lay
on my life, it was not really human life
but chemical, it was approximate landscape,
trenches and reaches, maybe it
was ordinary human life.
Now my mother sounds like me,
the way I sound to myself – one
who doesn't know, who fails and hopes.
And I feel, now, that I had wanted never to stop blaming her,
like eating hard-shelled animals
at mid-molt. But now my mother
is like a tiny, shucked crier
in a tide pool beside my hand. I think
I had thought I would falter if I forgave my mother,
as if, then, I would lose her – and I do
feel lonely, now, to sense her beside me,
as if she is only a sister. And yet,
though I hear her sighs close by my ear,
my mother is in front of me somewhere, at a distance,

moving slowly toward the end of her life,
the shore of the eternal – she is solitary,
a woman alone, out ahead
of everyone I know, scout of the mortal, heart
breaking into solo.

3. The Ecstatic

On her first antidepressant, my mother
is adorable. Like many of us, she's not
interested in much except herself, but these
days she's more happily interested
in herself. Now I think of those years with her
as the Middle Ages, before morphine.
We could have just put something in her food!
like a *Rose Fairy Book* potion. Yes, I
wanted her to put me first, I wanted
to draw out
Leviathan
with an hook. But I sensed the one under
the one under the spell – *this* one,
the child who was in there to be tinkered down to.
She's had her fitting for the MedicAlert,
'I've got it on, I'm all dingus'd up,
I knew you would want to know that I'm all
hooked up!' She is happy that I want to know,
and proud of wearing a little transmitter – not
unlike being an opera singer –
a link to those who wish her pleasure and long
life. Oh I have my mother on a leash.
Where wast thou, when I laid the foundations of the earth?
When the morning stars sang together?
I was there, with my mother.

4. Two Late Dialogues

MOM AS COMET

How do they know that it won't decide
to turn and come this way?! my mother,
at 82, points out. *They think*
they're soooo clever, giving it that funny
name no one can remember, but how do they
know that whatever's behind it won't suddenly
aim it at us? It's big, I mean
it's Oh-ho-HO! I see, I said,
yes . . . You think someone's running it? *Not*
SOMEONE, she scathed, *not a person: a force,*
a nameless force! But she could see that I did not
get it, that inhuman powers,
out of control, can kill you. So my mom,
who used to sleep with masking tape
stuck to her brow, to prevent wrinkles,
transmogrified her face, and became –
by slewing her mouth this way and that,
and rolling her eyes, and letting her head
wobble as her shoulders swayed back and forth
– Hale-Bopp. She looked like a comic actor
doing a drunk, she looked like a tough
kid on a corner, amusing the others,
a person with an identity,
who could play, enacting her own wild mother
veering toward her, or her father, falling
to his accidental death, or my father
lurching at her, or the wave of death
toppling her second husband, or her own
death, somewhere, its maw pulling
from side to side, its eyes unfocused,
hurtling toward her, an error, a horror – all
mimed with reckless energy, to astound and delight me.

HER CREED

I believe
in the creation of
the criminal,
the evil people,
my mother says on her eighty-third birthday,
everyone born is a miracle.
How did I know I would have YOU, she
cries out. 'I don't know what I would have done
without you, Mom,' I say, 'I'd still
be out there, calling MA–ma, MA–ma!'
She laughs with delight. But she's worried about cloning –
'When they clone *you,* Mom,' I tell her,
'I want one.' *I'll put you on the list,* she says.
'I want the little kind, that I can
put in a high chair and feed Cream of Wheat to,'
I add, and she says, *I'll move your name*
up high on the list. Over and over,
these days, she tells me they never will be able
to assemble real flesh, in a dish, not flesh
with spirit – the men cannot make happen
what happened in her body. When she dies, she wants to see
her father again, and put her arms
around her second husband. *Not a living*
cell with a soul. Oh – but Science,
she sighs, *you know –* 20,000
Leagues Under the Sea! 'Let's come back
and check on them,' I propose. 'On your birthday,
in the year 3000, I'll pick you up,
and we'll visit this planet.' *What will you be driving?*
she asks. 'A goose,' I tell my mother.
'I'll honk.' *Shave and a haircut*, she says.
They will never make flesh.

68

5. *Warily, Sportsman!*

> *Now the vast dusk bulk that is the whale's bulk . . .*
> *it seems mine,*
> *Warily, sportsman! though I lie so sleepy and*
> *sluggish, my tap is death.*
> 'The Sleepers,' Walt Whitman

When she talks about caring for her beloved husband
after his stroke, I hold the phone
in the crook of my shoulder, where the heads of sleeping
infants have rested. She goes over the heartaches
again, the setbacks, the bad nurse —
the one who was not professional,
who did not understand he was not
responsible for the things he said about her
race and about her neighborhood.
Suddenly, my mother bursts out,
And my therapist says it COULDN'T have been my
kicking him, the night before,
that caused the stroke. 'Of course not,'
I say, 'of course not. You, uh,
kicked him?' *He was sitting on the couch,*
we were fighting about which cruise to take next, I could
TELL how small the staterooms were
by the plan of the windows, but HE wanted to go
to RUSSIA, I kicked him in the shin with my soft
sneaker. And my doctor says that it had NOTHING
to do with the stroke or the cancer. I agree,
but a week later I stop short
on the street: my mother is still hitting and kicking people?
I know that soft sneaker. But when
she married again, I thought she'd stop hitting.
Or do people hit and kick each other
a lot, does everyone do it? Does each

family have its lineage
of pugilists? No one hit her back
until today – by-blow of this page,
coldcock to her little forehead.

6. Little End Ode

When I told my mother the joke — the new kid
at college who asked where the library's at,
and the sophomore who said, 'At Yale, we do not
end our sentences with prep-
ositions,' whereupon the frosh said, 'Oh,
I beg your pardon, where's the library
at, asshole' — she shrieked with delight.
Asshole, she murmured fondly. She's become
so fresh, rinsed with sweetness, as if she is
music, the strings especially high and bright.
She says it and sighs with contentment, as if she has
finally talked back to her own mother.
Or maybe it is the closest she has come,
for a while, to the rich, animal life
she lived with her second husband — now
I can see that of course she touched him everywhere,
as lovers do. She touched me there,
you know, courteously, with oil
like myrrh; soon after she had given me life
she gave me pleasure, which gave her pleasure,
maybe it felt to her fingertip like the
complex, clean knot of her Fire Girls
tie-clasp. She seems, these days, like a very
human goddess. I do not want her
to die. This feels like a new not-want,
a shalt-not-want not-want. As soon as I
dared, around fifty, I called her, to myself,
the A-word. And yet, now, if she goes,
when she goes, to me it is like the departure of a
whole small species of singing bird from the earth.

7. *Something Is Happening*

When it approaches, no one knows what it is – it is her
brain tumor, flaring up again.
My mother explains it to me – *Something
is happening, and it is physical,
and medical, and emotional,
and spiritual.* She's so sheerly lonely
she is like the one member of a tribe.
When she hears the doorbell – when it has not rung –
and she runs to it, she is like an explorer
of unseen deserts, unscanned rivers of
asteroids. Her naked body is almost
pretty, with its thousand puckers, maybe there's a
planet somewhere which holds this beaten-to
soft-peaks egg-white stomach the most
desirable. It was painful to know her,
such a feral one, untrained, unmothered,
but now she is playing at the edge of some field,
absorbed. There is something big coming,
bigger than love, bigger than aloneness.
She's staying up all night for it.
Something not an angel, not male or female,
is leaning on her brain. Up from within
the crease of the tumor, like the first appearance
of matter, something is arriving – not
her father, and not just death, but the truth,
her self, soon to be completed.

8. Cassiopeia

Just before dawn, the fixed stars
stand over my mother's house,
and the queen's throne seems to set
as the earth turns away from it.
But my mother is at her zenith — every
hour or so, these days, she stops talking,
and lets me have a turn, she squinches her
face like a child concentrating, she
knows this custom is important. Then
she is off again, on her long carouse
across the sky. There are two new
people who worship her. Well I worship you
myself, I say, for your good work
with the young musicians, and she says in her new
voice, Well I worship you right back.
Then she tells me the tumor may be growing again,
she has me finger the side of her radiant
visionary childhood face, to feel,
in the dent of her temple, the earth rising,
coming for her. She tells me her dream in which her
late husband, pissing in the goldfish
pool, turns toward her, laughing. She laughs,
her head thrown back, her hard palate
an arc, her curls gleaming like the moonlit
lake bush of an ancient Venus.
She was not meant to be a mother,
she never got to be a child until now —
I feel I am back in an early time,
when people were being tried out, combinations
of flowers, and animals, and hinges of iron,
and wheeling desire, and longing. I feel
like an old shepherd on a hill. My lamb,
who sickened so long, my first lamb, is gamboling.

PART FIVE
ONE SECRET THING

STILL LIFE

At moments almost thinking of her, I was
moving through the still life museum when my mother had her
stroke. I was with the furled leeks, I was
in the domain of the damp which lines
the chestnut hide, of dew on snails,
of the sweated egg, and the newts quick
and the newts gone over on their backs, and the withered
books — she was teaching someone, three
time zones away, to peel and slice
a banana, in the one correct way,
and I was wandering ruins of breakfasts,
broken crusts of a blackberry pie,
the leg of the paper wasp on it done
with a one-thread brush, in oil which had
ground gold in it. She had alerted me,
from the start, to objects, she had cried out
in pain, from their beauty, the way a thing
stood for the value of a spirit, an orange
trailing from its shoulders the stole of its rind,
the further from the tree, the more thinged and dried —
my mother was a place, a crossroads, she held the
banana and lectured like a child professor on its
longitudes and divisible threes,
she raised her hands to her temples, and held them,
and screamed, and fell to her bedroom floor, and I
wandered, calm, among oysters, and walnuts,
mice, apricots, coins, a golden
smiling skull, even a wild flayed
hare strung up by one foot like a dancer
leaping. There are things I will never know
about love. I strolled, ignorant
of my mother, among the tulips, beetle in its
holy stripes, she lay there and I walked
blind through music.

ONE SECRET THING

One secret thing happened
at the end of my mother's life, when I was
alone with her. I knew it should happen —
I knew someone was there, in there,
something less unlike my mother than
anything else on earth. And the jar
was there on the table, the space around it
pulled back from it, like the awestruck handmade
air around the crèche, and her open
mouth was parched. It was late. The lid
eased off. I watched my finger draw through
the jelly, its egg-sex essence, the four
corners of the room were not creatures, were not
the four winds of the earth, if I did not
do this, what was I — I rubbed the cowlick of
petrolatum on the skin around where the
final measures of what was almost not
breath swayed, and her throat made a guttural
creek bed sound, like pebbly relief. But each
lip was stuck by chap to its row
of teeth, stuck fast. And then I worked
for my motherhood, my humanhood, I
slid my forefinger slowly back and
forth, along the scab-line and underlying
canines and incisors, upper lip and then
lower lip, until, like a basted
seam, softly ripped, what had been
joined was asunder, I ran the salve in-
side the folds, along the gums,
common mercy. The secret was
how deeply I did not want to touch
inside her, and how much the act
was an act of escape, my last chance
to free myself.

THE LAST EVENING

Then we raised the top portion of the bed,
and her head was like a trillium, growing
up, out of the ground, in the woods,
eyes closed, mouth open,
and we put the Battle arias on, and when I
heard the first note, that was it, for me,
I excused myself from the death-room guests,
and went to my mother, and cleared a place
on the mattress, beside her arm, lifting
the tubes, oxygen, dextrose, morphine,
dipping in under them, and letting them
rest on my hair, as if burying myself
under a topsoil of roots, I pulled
the sheet up, over my head,
and touched my forehead and nose and mouth
to her arm, and then, against the warm
solace of her skin, I sobbed full out,
unguarded, as I have not done near her;
and I could feel some barrier between us dissolving,
I could feel myself dissolving it,
moving ever-closer to her through it, till I was
all there. And in her coma nothing
drew her away from giving me the basal
kindness of her presence. When the doctor came in,
he looked at her and said, 'I'd say
hours, not days.' When he left, I ate
a pear with her, talking us through it,
and walnuts – and a crow, a whole bouquet
of crows came apart, outside the window.
I looked for the moon and said, I'll be right
back, and ran down the hospital hall,
and there, outside the eastern window,
was the waxing gibbous, like a swimmer's head
turned to the side half out of the water, mouth

79

pulled to the side and back, to take breath,
I could see my young mother, slim
and strong in her navy one-piece, and see,
in memory's dark-blue corridor,
the beauty of her crawl, the hard, graceful
overhand motion, as someone who says,
This way, to the others behind. And I went back,
and sat with her, alone, an hour,
in the quiet, and I felt, almost, not
afraid of losing her, I was so
content to have her beside me, unspeaking,
unseeing, alive.

LAST HOUR

In the middle of the night, I made myself a bed
on the floor, aligning it true to my mother,
head to the hills, foot to the Bay where the
wading birds forage for mollusks – I lay
down, and the first death-rattle sounded
its desert authority. She had her
look of a choirboy in a high wind,
but her face had become matteryer,
as if her tissues, stored with her life,
were being replaced from some general supply
of gels and rosins. Her body would breathe her,
crackle and hearth-snap of mucus, and then
she would not breathe. Sometimes it seemed
it was not my mother, as if she'd been changelinged
with a being more suited to the labor than she,
a creature plainer and calmer, and yet
saturated with the yearning of my mother.
Palm around the infant crown of her
scalp where her heart fierce beat, palm to her
tiny shoulder, I held even with her,
and then she began to go more quickly,
to draw ahead, then she was still and her
tongue, spotted with manna spots,
lifted, and a gasp was made in her mouth,
as if forced in, then quiet. Then another
sigh, as if of relief, and then
peace. This went on for a while, as if she were
having out, in no hurry,
her feelings about this place, her tender
sorrowing completion, and then, against my
palm to her head, the resolving gift of no
suffering, no heartbeat;
for moments, her lips seemed to curve up –
and then I felt she was not there,

I felt as if she had always wanted
to escape and now she had escaped. Then she turned,
slowly, to a thing of bone,
marking where she had been.

TO SEE MY MOTHER

It was like witnessing the earth being formed,
to see my mother die, like seeing
the dry lands be separated
from the oceans, and all the mists bear up
on one side, and all the solids
be borne down, on the other, until
the body was all there, all bronze and
petrified redwood opal, and the soul all
gone. If she hadn't looked so exalted, so
beast-exalted and refreshed and suddenly
hopeful, more than hopeful – beyond
hope, relieved – if she had not been suffering so
much, since I had met her, I do not
know how I would have stood it, without
fighting someone, though no one was there
to fight, death was not there except
as her, my task was to hold her tiny
crown in one cupped hand, and her near
birdbone shoulder. Lakes, clouds,
nests. Winds, stems, tongues.
Embryo, zygote, blastocele, atom,
my mother's dying was like an end
of life on earth, some end of water
and moisture salt and sweet, and vapor,
till only that still, ocher moon
shone, in the room, mouth open, no song.

WHEN I LEFT HER

I remember the parting as if she had been
a gilded balsa crucifix, not
4' 11" but four and eleven-twelfths
inches, like a pale rattle a baby
could hold in her hand. Sometimes I look back and it's as
if I left a scepter lying
in the hospice bed, or a dowser of my mother,
but it was her body – although someone,
when my back had been turned, had laid her out
at parade rest,
her fleshless paws folded across her
goddess gate – pussycat,
where have you been? When I left her, she was at
stiff attention, beginning to warp
like outer space at its outer limits.
Feet start walking, something told
my feet, everyone was leaving, and I
deserted her, *I will not let thee*
go except thou bless me. Of course she had
blessed me – but while my legs went scissor-soft-
scissor, so that the butter walls
were melting past me, I could not count
my blessings, the feet that had stroked inside her
were being conveyed by the galilee floor toward the
door into night. It was like walking
away from someone who is drowning in inches
of water – and I'd bent beside her, and called to the
morphine to drown her, she had lain face up in the
cloud of it lowered like a pool to her face.
It was time. It was past midnight, the air of the
quiet town was wild with fresh salt
sea and pine. Never again.
Always. Never again. Always.

WESTERN WIND

Blowing from the Pacific — that pattern
piece of the globe's blue dress — blowing
from the Occident waters, from the Bay, from the tide flats,
the willet, heron, reed, mussel,
scallop, fault — at overcast dawn,
the western wind is bringing small,
dark clouds, up the slope
to the coastal hills dense with calcium
fog, and I wonder if any of the little
puffs is the smoke of my mother's flesh, from
the downwind crematorium
where her body lies this morning. When I saw it
last, it had diminished and hardened down
from what, at the end, had appeared to have become
a little singing sea on little
sea legs. The longer her body was dead,
the more it petrified — elkhorn,
kindling. This morning it bursts into High
C's of flame, this morning the complex
pastoral scene — nymph, trailing
diaphan, ibis, rill, pearl —
the solar system of my mother, the beauty of her
orbs, is fed, feet or head
first, into the Shadrach Meshach
Abednego, there to be divided
in two, the bed of gentle ash
rough with shards, radius and molars,
and the genies of buttery vapor, the fume
spirits — torn right through, in places,
showing the veery-egg blue — flying
slowly, low, up over the hills
on their way to the ice fields.

SATIN MAROON

In the narrow office on Shattuck and Ashby,
the woman pulled open a file drawer,
low tumble of wheels on rails,
and took out the ashes, in a satin maroon
plastic box, and set them on the desk.
Next of kin, I signed, and lifted them
up, and in the car I clasped her
tight, my arms seemed encircled around
the container twice, three times. Then I held her
up to my ear, and tilted her,
to hear whatever I could hear of her,
shirr of wisdom-teeth, of kiln bed
grit, dry mince like the crab-claws that she would
shuck to give us the brine-meat — gravel
rustle. The minister opened the chapel,
we set her where she'd always sat,
we put a rose beside her like
a petticoat. Then there she was,
on the sequoia pew, a magenta carton of
mortar-and-pestled bones. That it should
come to this. I kissed the smooth
surface, under which her silver
constellations turned, and then it was
time to leave her, overnight,
as we had planned, but it was hard to leave her
by herself, but suddenly, I saw
she had always been alone — fatherless,
mismothered — and not without her own
valiant spirit. And I wished she could descant
all night, as if this were she, this rattle of
salty campfire rubble from inside her,
and I left her there, I relinquished her
to the strangeness, the still home, of matter.

NEREID ELEGY

Early in the morning, we went through her garden,
filling bags with sempervirens,
sequoia, cedar, sugar pine, larch,
tearing each blown rose off its core,
dropping in cones, tiny lemons,
gardenia knobs, and the minister said,
Blessed are the Dead who Die in the Lord,
for they Rest from their Labors,
and we took the pint of her hearth-fluff to the Bay and cast
off into the fog. Cormorant, pelican,
tern, egret, whimbrel, we took her past
cliff and scoured-out tide tunnel,
staying in the lee of the mouth, and then we came
out, into chop and swell, like a rearing
horse on a heavy-seas carousel,
the boat was toward the open sea,
I pressed her square bucket of cinders
against my belly, the engine cut,
the prow swung slow around, the wind
dropped, and someone said, It's time.
And then I knew I was about to lose her,
she was going, there was no stopping it,
and it bent me over, Give Rest, O Christ,
to thy Servant, with thy Saints,
where Sorrow and Pain are no more, nor Sighing –
he held the box to me, and my mother
was violet-gray, she was blue spruce,
twilight, fur, I ran my hand into the
evening talcum of her absent action, and there
came, sharp up, with shards, and powders,
a tangle of circles soldered together,
the triple-strand wedding ring
from her finger touched me, now, on the other
side of the fire. I held it a moment

and then I loosed it overboard
in its damp puff of her parted flesh,
which blew in a cloud of starshine, and plunged
like milk into the water. Dust thou Art, and unto
Dust shalt thou Return, and he shook
the rest of her out, We Commit her Body
to the Deep. And we took the sack of blossoms and we
reached in, dropping brightness and limp
buoyant alloys in a trail above where her
rusts and corrids had gone, we laid down
a fresh path, we let her go,
we ushered her forth, like the death of a god,
the birth of an exhausted holiday.